Proceed with Caution

A Collection of Wee Stories

Walter Scott

ISBN
ScottSpace, Independent Publishing

For Correspondence Contact

walterscottpwc@gmail.com

Twitter: @WaltScott1

THIS BOOK IS DEDICATED TO THE
MEMORY OF PAUL AND GORDON

Imagine the laughs we could
have had with this,

til we meet again.

INTRODUCTION

Some people are natural storytellers, some are legends in their own heads, and some are masters of fairy-tale and myths. I have met all three many times over. The characters that you are about to meet in the following pages all have a story to share. They shared them with me, and I am sharing them with you.

The following tales contain a lot of swearing, and I mean a lot. So be warned. They also have a sprinkling of Scottish humour, some of it very dark. There's a little twist here and there that adds to the flavour. Hallucinogenic happenings bring unusual aspects to a couple of the tales. I'm hoping that at least one of the stories may bring a smile to your face, or maybe not; if one makes you feel sad or upset or connects with you in another way, then it's all good.

Raw, unfiltered, alcohol, drugs, darkness, and myth.

Enjoy.

CONTENTS

Introduction

1. SHUG AND HIS BINGE DRINKING

To Binge, or not to Binge?

The urge is so strong that Shug can feel it almost bursting through his veins. It all started with a few fleeting thoughts about six hours ago. The voice of a bewitching goddess whispering in his ear, seducing him with the ease and comfort that only she can bring.

'Have a drink, Shug; you know you want to.'

'C'mon Shug, a wee drinks no gonnae do you any harm.'

However, her sultry voice has gotten louder and louder; she is no longer enticing him. She is screaming at him relentlessly and now has complete control; it's all he can think about!

He tries to engage himself in other dialogue.

'Right, Shug, let's think about this. How long have you been on this health campaign, two weeks, two and a half? What the fuck? You can usually hold out for a bit longer than that. Jesus suffering fuck, where is this head fuck coming from?' I'm doing okay.

Shug...You're doing okay!'

Shug's desperately trying to pep talk himself, but it's a losing battle as all he can think of is getting on the swally. He needs a drink.

'The wife will fuckin kill me if she comes home from work and I'm out on another binge. That last binge... well, let's no even get into that, it still has me cringing, and the flashbacks are horrendous. C'mon tae FUCK Shug, get a grip of yourself here!' He's almost pleading with himself. Shug has a strong suspicion he's no gonnae make it...again! It's too strong, the power, the allure of the beverage. 'Think it through, Shug; you know it never goes to plan. You always end up fucked and making a complete cunt of yourself. Why would you want to do that again?'

BANG!

The front door slams behind him. He needs to get as far away from here as possible before his wife comes home.

'Right, whit's the plan maman?' Shug convinces himself that he's on to a winner if he has a plan. He needs to try something different this time rather than hanging around his usual haunts. 'I know, I'll head tae one of the local hotels; she'll never find me there.' He feels like a genius coming up with that idea.

'Fuck knows why she is still with you; you're a waste of space, look at the fuckin state of you.' The screaming banshee is back in his head.

'This binge stuff is a marriage wrecker, for sure.' Shug pushes those thoughts from his head and gets a spring in his step as he sees The Abbottsford Inn and Hotel. 'This should be far enough oot her way to get some peace.' He's pleased with himself. 'Not long now til my thirst can be quenched, and the binge can begin.'

(Having a blowout, or out on a binge as it's more commonly known, has been a problem of Shugs since his teens when he first started drinking. Shug has always been a binger. A binger is someone who, once they start drinking or once they've had a certain amount of booze, can't stop and don't stop until the adventure has run its course. They lose all control over conscious thought as they become possessed by the demon drink. Usually, it all ends in tears. That could mean anything from being found laying in the street with pish-stained trousers to waking up in jail or hospital, all accompanied by memory loss and heartache. Shug was a veteran of the binge, and this was the beginning of his latest breakout).

Hi there, do you have a room available for tonight?' Shug asks the receptionist.

'We certainly do, Sir, that will be sixty pounds.'

Shug thinks that's a bit steep but nods his head anyway before he asks if, as a resident, can he drink till late.

'You certainly can, Sir,' the receptionist replies. 'We will keep the bar open for as long as you keep ordering, all night if need be.'

'Ya fuckin beauty, I've hit the jackpot.' Shug does a wee dance in his head.

'There's your key, Sir. Enjoy your stay.'

Shug heads straight to the bar. 'A pint of lager barman, please,' he smiles as the barman hands him his pint. 'Thank you very much.' The binge is on.

After a few pints, Shug decides to view his room, maybe have a shower, freshen up for the evening ahead and put what little possessions he has with him in a safe place while he gets fucked out his barnet with booze. As he enters the room, the phone rings; Shug thinks, 'What the fuck?' He answers the phone to discover that it's his wife on the other end.

'Shug, please do not do this again; we've spoken about this bingeing; please come home, at least do it in the house, and we can try to contain it, please.' She is almost begging him.

He can't handle hearing the exasperation in her voice, so he disconnects. It's game on; no going back now. A new plan is required. 'I'll change hotels; that will buy me some time.' Again, he is impressed by his genius thinking. After gathering his possessions, he heads out to find another hotel to continue with his adventure.

While strolling down the street, the few pints he's

had start to kick in, and he's feeling pretty good. 'Ah, this is the life, footloose and fancy-free.' He sees The Dumbuck Hotel and feels like an excited schoolboy. 'This will do nicely,' he says out loud.

'Good evening, Sir.' The receptionist greets him.

'I'd like a room for the night.' says Shug.

'No problem, Sir, that will be sixty-five pounds.'

Shug pays and thinks the extra fiver is worth it if it keeps the wife from finding him. He heads straight to the bar.

'Pint of lager please and a whisky chaser.' 'Lovely,' he thinks as he knocks back the chaser. Shug enjoys his drink and starts up a conversation with the barman.

'If you've booked a room in here, can you drink all night?'

'Not in here, mate,' the barman replies. 'I know some local hotels do that, but we only keep the bar open til two.'

'Oh fuck,' thinks Shug, 'I'd better get a carry-oot for the room as I'll still be wanting to drink way beyond that.'

Shug heads to the shop and buys enough booze to keep him going through the night. He's not thought much further ahead than that.

Returning to the hotel with his cargo, he heads upstairs to view his new room and stash his booze in anticipation for later. He enters the room; it looks lovely. The phone rings. 'What the fuck?' thinks Shug. He answers the phone. It's his wife again.

'Shug, please do not do this; we've spoken about this bingeing; please come home at least do it in the house, and we can try to contain it, please.'

'What the fuck?' Shug is bewildered and a bit freaked out. He shouts down the phone.

'How the fuck are you able to track and find me in these hotels?'

His wife shouts,

'I'm phoning your mobile, ya drunk prick. Now get up the fuckin road!'

2. CHOCOLATE SURPRISE

There's the door.

It's my recorded delivery, lovely jubely.

I've been waiting in anticipation, wondering what's gonnae be in my goody box. I'd been on the app called Massroots, where you connect with others who are fond of all things weed-related. I'm not that into weed; it always makes me feel quite uncomfortable, and it can make me very paranoid as well as ravenously hungry. Sometimes I've ended up stuffing pizza into my mouth while wondering how many people are talking about me and in what way. Although every so often, I think to myself, it's time to give it another go. I like how it affects others that I know; they absolutely love it. They seem so chilled out on it, so relaxed, and able to function in a wonderfully mellow way. I want that feeling rather than the paranoid android that I can become. So, it's time to have another blast at it to see if I can achieve the mellow feeling I'm after. This time I've decided to try infused edibles, sweet things like cake and jelly sweeties.

The smoking doesn't seem to agree with me, so we'll

see how we go with the edibles.

I sign for the recorded delivery and take my pizza-shaped box up into the kitchen. I place it on the table and gently cut the tape loose, then slowly open the box to reveal my wee selection of infused treats. Mmmmmmm, a selection of five treats to choose from, hard-boiled sweets, gummy bear-type things, two lollies, and a piece of what looks like sticky toffee pudding with a serving of chocolate sauce.

What to try first?

I read the small handwritten instructions accompanying the treats—details about heating the sticky toffee pudding with a serving of chocolate sauce. The recommendation is not to eat it all at once unless you are a seasoned stoner type. Well, I'm certainly not a seasoned stoner, so I will proceed with caution. I decide to choose the sticky pudding over the other treats as it already smells amazing.

Ok, here we go; the instructions say how long to heat it in the oven, and if that's what they say, that must be what's to happen. Also, heat the sauce in a pot. I don't have a cooker; I'm not big on the whole cooking thing. I've got a microwave, but the instructions say to heat in a proper oven for the cake and boil the sauce in a wee pot.

Firstly, a wee bit of background here to set the scene. I live above my mother; she's in her 70's, still independent, and does her thing. I give her a hand with anything troubling her without interfering too much—a Granny flat type set up. As people get older, they still like their independence, and rightly so, you've gotta be careful not to overstep the mark while making sure they are doing just fine.

Anyways, she has a cooker.

I take my sticky toffee pudding with side serving of chocolate sauce and head down to my mother's section. I give the door a wee knock.

'Alright, Maw, what's happening?'

'Not much happening tonight son, I'm just watching a wee bit of telly.'

'Marvellous,' says I. 'I need to use your cooker to heat a wee cake I've purchased if that's alright, Maw?'

'Aye son, on you go, help yersel, mind tidy up efter yersel,' she shouts.

Lovely, let's get this cooker up and running.

It all seems pretty straightforward, set the oven to the correct temperature, bung in the cake, keep an eye on the time as I heat the chocolate sauce in a wee pot. I'm parading about the kitchen like Gordon fuckin Ramsay, and it's a canter this cooking lark. In all honesty, though, fuck that, cooking and kitchens and preparing food just isn't my thing. However, this is a wee bit of fun.

Everything seems to be going to plan, and I'm keeping an eye on the time for the cake. The sauce is already in its pot. We're almost there. A wee buzzer goes on the cooker, and time's up. The cake is ready. I carefully take the cake out and plate it up. Now I gently pour the chocolate sauce over the cake and, hey presto, it's good to go. The cake and sauce are extremely hot, so I tidy up after myself while giving it a chance to cool.

'Right, let's go,' I say to myself as I lift my culinary delight and head out of my Maw's kitchen. I give her living room door a wee knock.

'Maw, that's me did my thing, and I've tidied up efter masel. I'll maybe check back in with you later; if not, then I'll see you tomorrow, ok?'

'Hold on a minute, son, what's that lovely smell? Whatever you've been making in there smells bloody amazing.'

I enter her living room carrying my cannabis-infused cake.

'I've been heating this wee cake Maw, as I hud a notion for some chocolate, you know how it gets you sometimes.'

'Aye a dae son, I know exactly how it gets ye sometimes, I could fair go some chocolate maself, and that smells lovely. Huv ye got enough to share?'

I look at my old Maw sitting there, just chilling watching some telly, an I think, 'What to do here?' The note that came with this said you`ve gotta be careful as it can be very strong.

The devil on one shoulder is saying to me, 'Just give it tae the crabbit auld bastard, sort her right oot!' The character on my other shoulder mumbles something that I can't make out.

'Here you go, Maw, fill yer boots.'

I pass her the cake...

I sit down and watch her shovel the cake into her mouth. The lovely sticky toffee pudding and chocolate sauce look like they're hitting the spot. She doesn't pause for breath. Her gluttonous tendencies have gotten the better of her, and she can't be stopped. It's carnage as she devours the cannabis cake like some soulless demon. I'm watching the performance of the cake monster thinking to myself, you greedy mother fucker, hell scud it intae ye. If she would slow down a little bit, she may even taste the cannabis. But no, no slowing down as she gets whipped into a chocolate frenzy. She's almost halfway through the cake and sauce when she suddenly stops eating. Slowly turns to me and says,

'Is that fuckin weed I can taste?'

I can't contain myself, and the laughter explodes from me; I'm struggling to answer her.

'Aye, says me, 'It's fuckin infused with cannabis ya greedy fucker.'

My mother hasn't exactly led a sheltered life and is well acquainted with the world of weed.

'Get this tae fuck away from me, you sick bastard,' she screams.

She's probably right, there may well be an element of sick bastard involvement here, but one couldn't help oneself, and what's done is done. I take the remains from her and back away.

'You're a fuckin prick,' she's shouting.

I'm no hearing the tirade of abuse she's directing at me as I'm pissing myself wi laughter.

I retreat with what remains of the cake and head back up the stair to my abode. I get myself comfortable, stick my tv on, light a candle, and prepare for what I'm hoping is a relaxing time that brings the mellow feeling that I'm after. I plan to stick a movie on and just chill out.

I eat the remains of the cake. It is absolutely delicious; I can understand why my Maw was enjoying it so much.

Getting myself settled on the couch, I start to channel hop, hoping to find a movie that looks interesting, and if nothing is happening, I'll try Netflix.

About half an hour or so has passed, and I've not been able to find anything on TV or Netflix that's grabbed my attention. Although I am starting to feel nice and relaxed. I seem to be feeling that mellow way I was after, and all is well. I decide to pick a channel on tv and just let it run. I'm not that bothered it seems about tuning into a movie.

More time passes. How much more time passes, I'm not sure. All I know is that I'm getting more and more fuckin stoned. I mean, it just isn't slowing down. I'm way past the mellow chilled-out feeling that I was after. I'm starting to get a wee tad worried as it just won't stop getting stronger and stronger. (I remember eating some weed or a piece of solid dope from the past and ending up hallucinating).

'Oh god, I wish this would stop;' it's too strong for me. I can hardly move; my mouth is as dry as a stick, and I can't get up for something to drink. My vision is starting to get a bit weird. The tv is sounding a little odd. I know deep down that this shit is too powerful for an inexperienced stoner like me. It feels like I'm close to entering some sort of hallucinogenic experience. 'Please God, no, I'm no in the mood for this kinda shit.'

I don't know how much time is passing as I don't know much anymore. I'm fucked out of my mind.

Suddenly an advert on TV grabs my attention. Oak Furnishing. 'What the fuck?' 'Who gives a fuck about Oak Furnishing?' Some guy is staring at me from the screen, straight at me. He's talking directly to me; how the fuck is that possible? His big staring eyes. He looks right at me an says,

'There's no veneer, in here.'

'Oh, help me, Lord.' I've rolled off the couch with laughter. I've no idea why this is the funniest thing ever. 'There's no veneer in here; what the fuck's so funny?' I don't know, but I'm laughing so much that it's becoming painful, and my mouth is becoming even drier, if that's possible. 'Oh, dear God, help me. This is way beyond mellow.'

Stronger and stronger the feeling gets. I'm starting to worry a bit, praying that it will begin to wear off. I've lost all track of time. I hear a noise in the distance, and it's getting louder and louder. It's my phone, where is it? The ring tone seems to bring some clarity as if the weed has taken a time-out. I don't know, something clicks, and I'm able to answer the phone.

'What the fucks happening up there?' My brother shouts down the phone at me. 'I've just had Maw on the phone mumbling incoherently about cigarettes and pizza. She sounds like she's having a fuckin stroke or something.'

'Fuck. I'd forgotten about my Maw eating the cake earlier.'

I attempt to answer my brother, but it turns out that I'm also mumbling incoherently. I disconnect and push the phone away from me. I somehow manage to turn myself over. Christ knows how long I've been laying on the floor?

I'm now ravenous with hunger and attempt to crawl through to my kitchen. It feels like I'm moving in slow motion. It's hard work as I gradually ease myself toward my fridge. The hunger I feel is incredible. I must eat.

(In the world of weed and being stoned, I have a severe case of the 'munchies')

I open the fridge to find all I have is a tub of Stork margarine. I read the label which says,

GOOD ENOUGH FOR CAKES.

Well, if it's good enough for cakes, then it's damn well good enough for me.

I'm stoned out of my mind and must eat something. With some difficulty, I manage to get the lid off. I use two fingers and scoop some margarine into my mouth.

At this point, something miraculous happens. The margarine tastes like marzipan. I can't believe it. I'm in marzipan heaven. I've hit the jackpot. The smooth texture just melts in my mouth. I`m amazed as to why I didn't know this?

Filled with happiness, I munch away at my delicacy.

It feels like fireworks of delight dancing over my tastebuds...

'Haw you? What the fuck ye up tae?'

And there's my brother standing at the door.

I think to myself, 'How did he do that? One minute he's on the phone, and the next thing you know, he's right there. Is he able to time-travel? Oooooft, this stuff is strong.'

He sees the box of edibles and quickly grasps the situation. Well, he seems to understand what's going on with me. He's yet to find out that Maw's eaten them too.

He takes the margarine off me and helps me to my feet, and then on to a chair.

'What the fucks happened to Maw,' he asks.

I'm a little more coherent by this point and somehow manage to tell him the story of the edibles and Maw wanting a wee taste of chocolate.

'Fuck's sake, brother,' he says, 'That's a bit heavy. When I came in there, I honestly shit myself as I thought she was deed man!'

It turns out he wasn't sure what to do when he'd first arrived. He'd gotten a bit of a fright when he found his Maw comatose. He thought that she was dead. (I know it's bad). When he had come in, he'd found Maw completely unconscious and unresponsive. He'd panicked because there was just nothing, and in his panicked state, he couldn't find her pulse. That's how bad things had gotten that he felt the need to check for a pulse. He had put his phone screen to her nose and mouth to see if any vaper was coming out. That's what he did. I don't think I would have thought of that?

'She had slumped back in the chair, her head was hanging over backwards, her mouth was wide open, and she was a kinda light green colour. Fuck knows how her head was managing to tilt so far backwards; that's gonnae hurt when that weed wears off man. Once I put my phone to her face and saw that vapour was coming out and knew she was breathing, I relaxed a little but still almost phoned for an ambulance.' 'Thank fuck I didnae. Can you imagine?'

'What's wrong with my Maw?'

'Well, Sir, we have to inform you that yer Maw is fuckin stoned oot her tiny napper, and what we suggest is fluid and loads ay pizza to aid her recovery.'

He tells me that he's managed to sit her up properly and put a pillow behind her neck.

'Don't get me wrong,' he laughs, 'Once I knew that she was alive, I couldn't resist taking a picture of her predicament; it was quality. I've never seen her like that. When she's feeling a bit better, I'll show her the picture and tell her, "Just say no to drugs."'

We are certainly seeing the funny side of this.

'C'mon down the stairs, and we'll make sure all is well.'

We go down and check on our Maw, who has come around a little, not much, though. We give her some juice and help her to bed, where she spends the next two days sleeping off the effects of the weed-infused cake. When she does come around, she says that was one of the best sleeps ever—a tad thirsty when she eventually awakens but a great sleep all the same.

For me, well, after my brother leaves, I also go to my bed and fall into a deep sleep. I sleep till morning (unlike my mother's two days), and when I awaken, I have a wee swatch in the mirror. You can tell that I'm still not entirely functioning properly. It's in the eyes. My eyes are still all bloodshot and swollen, and it's a day for the house. Definitely not a day for driving. Plus, my stomach is aching from eating that disgusting margarine!

Is there a message within this story about drugs or morals, or boundaries? I don't know? Make your own mind up. It makes me think about Forest Gump and his box of chocolates.

'Life is like a box of chocolates,' he says. 'You don't know what you're getting next.'

But I know for sure that if he had picked a cannabis-infused one, he wouldn't have been so keen on the running bit.

'Run Forest Run.'

'Fuck off,' says he, and 'Get me some pizza.'

PROCEED WITH CAUTION

3. BILLY CONNOLLY AND IVAN THE TERRIBLE

Many years ago…more than I like to think of, the phone goes.

'Do you want to be an extra in a movie?'

I'd joined the real people casting agency and was getting offered a job.

'Sure,' I said. 'What's the details?'

'It's called *The Debt Collector* and will be starring Billy Connolly.'

'That sounds just fuckin marvellous,' I thought.

I'd always wanted to meet him, and this was the perfect opportunity. I'd heard various stories about him over the years, and a couple of the stories were quite close to home. Maybe I'd get to meet him and have a wee chat.

We go along to filming, my sister Pauline was with me, I'd managed to get her involved. I told her there was a day's pay, in cash – that sealed the deal! On arriving at the film location, we're ushered into this large holding area where I notice a full kilt out-fit hanging up, with my name on it; 'Seems promising,'

I thought.

Next thing I know.

` Alright, you're going to be involved in a scene later, so get the kilt outfit on and make your way to the marque.'

We head along to the wedding scene being shot in the big tent and find ourselves some seats. It's time to get comfy for what could be a long, dull day of filming.

A few hours pass and the boredom is setting in. Pauline and I had been sitting playing cards to help pass the time when we noticed some changes in the scene. 'Ok, what's going on here?' It turns out that the next scene was gonnae involve me doing something. 'Bring it on,' I thought.

I receive more direction.

'When Billy shouts at Ken Stott, "Hey Kelty ya bastard," and follows him out to attack him, you come out behind and pull Billy off of Ken".

'Sounds fair enough,'

This was it, my brush with fame.

We do a couple of takes. After each take, we get dried off as the fake rain is soaking us through. We're about to head out for the third take, and Billy turns to me an says,

'I'm gonnae fuckin go for this wee tussle, get right in about it.'

'All right, Billy, you do what the fuck you think's right. I've been involved in competitive wrestling my whole life, started when I was five years old at the Milngavie wrestling club. So, fill yer boots.'

I was buzzing; I'd got to speak with him. We had a conversation – well, that's how it felt to me. I had got to say what I'd wanted to say, and I wondered if it had registered with him?

TAKE 3...

...AND ACTION!

We go for it.

Billy goes for it.

'Kelty ya bastard!'

Billy storms after him outside the marque an jumps Ken. I'm there, I pull Billy off and it's a rap. The scene is done. My brush with fame is over.

I'm drying myself off after the scene's completion when Billy comes over,

'Can I have a wee word with you in private?'

'Ya fuckin dancer,' thinks I; 'He must have heard what I'd said.'

'See earlier when we were gonnae shoot that scene, and you started wi the wrestling patter,'

'Aye.'

'You know all about it, don't you?'

'Aye, a dae.' (I'd said it in the hope that this wid happen)

'Do you know Joe?'

'I know him to say hello to; I'm more connected with his younger brother John through the wrestling. John helped coach me back in the day.'

'Fuck John,' he says. 'Do you know how close me and Joe were?'

'Yip, I'd heard a few stories about all the parties with you, some Celtic players, and all sorts of famous movers and shakers. Legendary stories from they times.'

'Do you know what happened the last time Joe an I spoke?'

'Yeh, I know.'

(We discussed what had gone on the last time Billy and Joe had met. That's a private matter).

'Right, are you gonnae bump into Joe any time soon?'

'Aye, I'll go down The Black Bull Bar; He's in there quite regularly for a couple of pints.'

'Ok, here's a message for him.' *"Joe, you're a wee bastard."* 'Have you got that clear now?'

'Aye, It's pretty straightforward, Billy. *"Joe, you're a wee bastard."*

'Ok then, you give him that message, and I'll see you around the set.' So off goes Billy.

I look up to see all the nosey bastards wondering what the fuck that had been about?

A couple of days pass, and I'm heading down to The Black Bull Bar to see Joe. There he's seated.

'All right, Joe, I've got a message from an old friend of yours,'

'Oh aye, who?'

'It's from your old best mate, Billy.'

'What does that fucker want?' asks Joe.

'He doesn't want fuck all bar me passing on a message to you.'

"*You're a wee bastard.*"

'That's the message, Joe.'

I tell Joe all about being an extra on *The Debt Collector,* and the details of the lengthy conversation me an Billy had. Joe adds to the stuff Billy had been talking about, talks about how close they had been, then never to speak again from that fateful day. For me, it was fuckin great. I was getting to hear how things had been back in the day, listening to stories about Billy and Joe when Joe ran a couple of clubs in Glasgow and cruised about in his Jenson Interceptor.

'Anyway,' Joe says, 'When are you likely see that fucker again?'

'I'm hoping to get a few more days filming quite soon,' says I.

'Okay, give him this message.'

I never did get to give Billy the return message as I didn't see him again.

(*While writing this, I bumped into John, Joe's younger brother, who told me that Joe had passed away the previous week*).

I've still got that message for Billy; if he ever wants it, I'm easy to find.

When I met Joe's young brother the other day and he was telling me about Joe dying; we got onto the subject of Billy and his close friendship with Joe.

John recalled the story of when there had been a woman at one of Joe's parties who didn't like Billy, for whatever reason? The woman was on Billy's case all fuckin day; he just couldn't catch a break from her. How she thought he was so far up his own arse, who the fuck did he think he was, a fuckin upstart. She was there with her husband, a famous Celtic player at the time. As the party gathered momentum and the drink flowed, the insults just kept getting worse – nothing would shut this woman up. Billy decides to go to the toilet to get away from her for a bit.

He's away for a few minutes and then slowly makes his way back into the main room of the house, where the party is in full swing. The woman spots him, and she goes for the jugular with the insults; he can't take any more of this fuckin crazy woman. So... he flies for her, arms outstretched, lunging for her. Fuck knows what he thought was gonnae happen when he reached her? (It was never gonnae happen anyway with Joe's younger brother John around. John is a formidable man of short height. He is an Olympic wrestler, competed at the Mexico Olympics, not to be fucked with, short though, five feet, one, maybe.)

John starts to get animated as he continues recalling the story.

'I jump on Billy and wrestle him to the ground, where I use a couple of wrestling moves an tie him up. Billy's fuckin an effin an all the bastards. His face had turned bright red, an he's swearin an blindin an fuckin slabberin. It doesn't take long til Billy realises he's not going anywhere; I've got him trussed up like a chicken.

Then suddenly, it all changes. Billy just starts laughing, uncontrolled laughter, like a madman.'

John says, 'To this day, looking back, I still admire how quick he was with the humour when he shouted,'

"Now I know how Gulliver fuckin felt when the little people tied him up!"

John says, 'The place erupted with laughter, and it was like something from a comedy show. The tension left the room, I helped Billy back to his feet, me an him were fine with each other, the woman had fucked off, and on went the party.'

A few days later. Billy's back out at Joe's.'That was some party, Joe, sorry about that wee bit of nonsense with the daft woman who wouldn't leave me the fuck alone.'

'No worries, Billy, sorry about my brother maybe being a wee bit rough on you.'

'Don't be daft, Joe; it's given me a bit of an idea for a good story that I could maybe use in my act. When your young brother John had me down and tied up like a chicken, he had my body bent double with all that wrestling stuff. At one point, my face was buried into his crotch; I thought about sinking my teeth intae his Wullie. It turns oot; it was my ain fuckin crotch, he had me bent double and twisted right roon, the wee bastard, so, I'd have bit my ain fuckin Wullie.' Great material though Joe, I'm thinking Russian wrestler Ivan the Terrible and the amazing strength he gets oot biting his ain Wullie…'

And the rest is history.

If you're not familiar with Billy and his Ivan the Terrible story from back in the day, there are worse things you could do with your time than searching it out!

WALTER SCOTT

4. SQUARE GO
THE BABOON

'That'll be right! You've got a baboon kept in a storage container?'

James is having a conversation with some travellers he's just met in a bar in Glasgow's Southside.

'A fuckin baboon, you jokin?'

They weren't fuckin jokin. Ian, the leader of the crew, explains to James the ins and outs of owning a baboon. (How they ended up with a baboon is for another time).

Ian explains that they're trying to think of ways to make some money with it, or they`re just gonnae end up shooting it.

'The plan is,' says Ian, 'We're gonnae find some mad bastards who think they're as hard as fuck to fight the baboon. The winner takes the purse. We'll put up ten grand; the mad hard bastard and his crew put up ten grand. The rules are no weapons allowed; you go in the container, fight the baboon. You either knock the thing out, or you shout to be let out of the cage. It's that simple, and we hear that you're the man to see as you have connections to the dark side of life. You've got a finger in all the pie's as they say. What we would like from you is to go round all your connections and find out if any of them have, in amongst their muscle, anyone mad enough to fight a fuckin baboon for ten grand?'

James is well connected with the underworld of Glasgow. He's been involved in that sort of thing his whole life. He does know a man who knows a man who can get you whatever illegal thing takes your fancy but finding someone to fight a baboon; this was a new one. 'I'll need to watch how I approach this, or people will think I'm losing my mind,' thinks James.

Firstly, he decides to visit the local boxing gym. He's got a few friends and contacts there. It's a busy evening at the boxing training, and the club is packed. James spots his good friend Alex.

'Alright, Alex, my friend, much happening tonight?'

'Just another busy night at the boxing, same old. What about yourself, what you up to?'

'Nothing much,' says James, 'Just floating about. I've got the possibility of a wee prize fight if any of the boys might be interested?'

'You know we don't entertain that kind of stuff in here James, what's brought you here to ask me that, you know the score!'

'Well, this is a wee bit different, Alex. I'm no even sure how to put it to you?'

'James, just tell me what it is. I've got a busy night here.'

'Alright Alex, do any of the boys fancy a prize-fight for a ten grand purse?'

'Ten fuckin grand, who the fuck have they got to fight?'

'Well, this is where it gets a bit odd. It's no who they have to fight; it's what? They would have to fight a baboon in a container. I'm just telling you how it is; that's what it is, fight a baboon in a container.'

'James, get the fuck out of here now. I don't know what's up wi you; go and get some help. You're getting worse, now fuck off!'

James fucks off.

'That didn't go well at all,' thinks James. 'Maybe this baboon thing is gonnae be more problematic than I first thought. Well, I knew it wisnae normal, but, fur fucks sake, it's not that strange, is it?' As he's strolling along the main road, it just so happens he fancies a couple of pints and heads to his local bar. James orders a pint and retreats to a quiet spot in the corner. 'Who the fuck can I find that would be up for fighting a baboon and allowing me to collect my finder's fee from the mad travellers?'

Just at that, the pub door opens, and in walks Mad Stevie. Mad Stevie is well known locally; in fact, Mad Stevie is well-known all over Glasgow. His reputation as a hard bastard has been well established for some years now. He's seen off plenty pretenders to his throne of being the maddest bastard around. These days most people just accept that this crazy fucker, is just a crazy fucker.

James can't remember if the mad bastard is now associating with a particular crew or gang; from what he can remember, Stevie was always freelance, ready to do some poor bastard if the money was right. Maybe? Just maybe, this is the man for the job?

James approaches him where he's standing at the bar.

'Alright, Stevie, how's tricks?'

'How you doin James? What's happening?'

'Well, Stevie Boy, I just recently had an interesting conversation with some travellers, and they've asked me to help them out with something. That something is a bit fuckin nutty, to say the least. However, it is what it is. When I saw you come in there, I thought, "Stevie, might just be the man to point me in the right direction with this."'

'You shouldn't get fuckin mixed up with they travellers; you know they're all fuckin mad?' Hearing Stevie call someone mad almost put me into a fit of laughing; I kept it in though, I value my life!

'Aye Stevie, I hear what you're sayin,' but it was an interesting proposition they had.'

'Ok, tell me what it is, an I'll tell ye if I can help you with it?'

'Mind noo,' says James, 'It was the travellers who put this to me! They've got a fuckin baboon kept in a storage container, and they're wanting to put its fighting skills to the test. It's an old thing. According to them, there's no much life left in the poor fucker. With the offer of a wee finder's fee, they've asked me to find someone tae fight it. Ten grand put down by the travellers, and ten grand put down by the challenger, winner takes all.'

Stevie seemed to listen to every word, and now there was a pause. Was this mad bastard gonnae go for it?

'I'll fight the fucker,' says Stevie, then takes a swig of his pint as if he's just agreed to a game of fives. This fuckin lunatic was gonnae go for it. Game on.

As soon as I'm up the road, I'm on the phone with Ian, leader of the crew. Ian's delighted, and we agree on a date, a week on Saturday for the big fight. Cash money to be brought along on the day of the fight. Money to be held by a neutral and presented to the winner, no fuckin about. I then phone Stevie, tell him a week on Saturday, cash money, no fuckin about, winner takes all. And that was that. That was how the weirdest fuckin thing I've ever been involved in came about...

FIGHT DAY

James makes his way down to the yard on fight day. What mayhem was gonnae take place today was anybody's guess. He'd heard that Mad Stevie hadn't been near the pub, and the crazy bastard had been seen out joggin like a fuckin lunatic.

The place is mobbed. There must be about a hundred travellers, all fuckin mental, all eager to bet on the outcome once they've eyed up Stevie.

James spots Ian and walks over for a wee catch-up of what the plan is. Ian explains that once Stevie and whatever gang he's taken up with arrive, there will be a quick run-through of the rules. The boys can all get a look at Stevie, and the bets can start to change hands. Sounds fair enough.

Just at that moment, Mad Stevie arrives; he's with Tam and his crew. Tam must have taken on Stevie as his man, putting the money up. Tam and Ian have a wee chinwag, and the money is handed to the neutral, who takes a seat to count through the cash. At this point, the noise and excitement are starting to build. The travellers are passing the drink around, and joints are being smoked, coke is being snorted. They're here to enjoy the spectacle. Mad Stevie is being encouraged to strip to the waist, as the boys wanna see what he's made of.

'C'mon bigchap, let's fuckin see what you've got.'

Stevie strips off and starts to stretch and warm-up. He starts some shadow boxing, showing his speed and footwork. In all fairness, Stevie is in good shape, and he can move. The travellers can see that this man is no mug. There's plenty of betting taking place, and from what I can gather, Stevie has made a good impression as some of the bets are going on him for a win. I'm just praying that whatever's gonnae happen is gonnae happen without too much trouble. Tam and his gang will be carrying weapons, for sure.

Then the moment arrives for the unveiling of the baboon, and Ian pulls the container doors open.

I can't believe what I'm seeing. The baboon is a monster, a big, huge fuckin male in the prime of its life, well looked after and bristling with animal aggression. It is one formidable-looking scary mother fucker with two big fangs. I'm scared of this thing. It's bouncing about in its cage, sensing something is gonnae be taking place. Surely tae fuck Stevie's no gonnae go through with this?

Stevie is surrounded by Tam an his gang of about twenty men, and they're helping him stretch off and offering words of encouragement. Stevie's staring over at the cage, eyeing up his opponent.

'Ten more minutes for betting,' shouts Ian; 'Then the fight will begin.'

The time ticks by as all bets are placed. Then a voice roars:

'Time gentlemen, no more bets. Let's get ready tae rumble, as they say.'

The crowd surrounds the entrance to the container; it's on a large platform, a few feet up, easy for all to see the action. Stevie steps forward and walks toward the cage where Ian is waiting to let him in. Stevie's worked up a good sweat and looks like he's gonnae give this his best shot. Ian asks him if he's ready.

The baboon is going fuckin mental, swinging about, bangin things, screaming; its fangs look horrifying. This is, indeed, a wild, ferocious animal. Ian unlocks the section where the food gets put, and Stevie steps in. He's on his own now, and it's up to him to slide back the panel and enter the main section to start the fight. Ian locks the door behind Stevie.

Stevie takes a deep breath, slides back the panel, and enters the main section. Time stands still; everything goes silent. The baboon is frozen to the spot, its evil stare penetrating Stevie.

BOOM!

It's on Stevie, teeth sunk right into his shoulder. Stevie's screaming in agony as he's punching it in the head. He breaks free and catches the baboon with a ferocious shot to the face, thumb right into the baboon's eye. It's stunned and steps back in retreat. The crowd let up a big cheer, game on. The baboon comes at him again, screaming, screeching, fangs glistening in the light. It swipes at Stevie and tears a large piece of flesh from his face; you can see his jawbone exposed.

Stevie's fuckin enraged. They lock together and roll

along the cage floor. I can't believe what I'm see-ing. Stevie has now sunk his teeth into the baboon's face and is tryin tae tear off the baboon's flesh. This is fuckin nuts. The crowd is in a frenzy, shout-ing, screaming. The baboon lets out some kind of scream, a noise I can't explain, animalistic, dark, evil. Stevie fights to his feet and staggers back. He's not looking good!

One of his eyes is hangin loose, dangling by some threads, or whatever it is that holds your eyes in. It's a horror show now. Someone shouts,

'Get him the fuck out of there before that thing kills him.'

Stevie reaches up and pushes his eye back into place. As he does this, the baboon screams in a high pitch of evil and lunges at Stevie. Stevie reaches into the back of his trousers and pulls out what looks to be a knife. The crowd has completely lost it by now, and everyone is screaming,

'Get Stevie out!'

Then they see the knife that Stevie has pulled out from the back of his trousers. As the baboon comes at him, Stevie stabs it in the face. The knife must have been about 8 inches long, and only the handle is now visible; he has embedded it right up to the hilt. Ian, the leader of the travellers, is furious, and he's shouting,

'You dirty bastard, no fuckin weapons.'

The baboon has fallen backward and is obviously dying, the blade penetrating right through to its brain. It's screeching and screaming some death noise. It's painful listening to this horrifying tone. Then the baboon goes quiet. The crowd go quiet, stunned. No one can believe what they have just witnessed. Ian breaks the silence,

'I fuckin told you no weapons, you bastard,' he unlocks the cage and pulls Stevie out.

Now we have a situation.

Stevie has stabbed the baboon, and it's dead. The rules were no weapons. Someone's not getting ten grand. Tam and his crew of about twenty men are told, in no uncertain terms, to fuck off. Tam has enough sense and some understanding of self-preservation. He signals to his men that it's time to leave. Mad Stevie doesn't get to leave. He broke the rules and will be dealt with, traveller style...

Although a few years have passed since this incredible tale took place. The legend of Mad Stevie lives on. His exploits and legacy gathering momentum. He's become something of a cult hero in these parts and adding to the folklore surrounding him is the fact that he was never seen again after the fight with the baboon. Rumour has it that Stevie decided to lead the life of a traveller and moved away with them to pastures new.

However, if, for some crazy reason, a team of

archaeologists are digging in that old yard in the future. They may, just maybe, come across a human skeleton in a loving embrace with a baboon, and that will give them something to think about...

5. MARTIN AND THE DT'S

Martin has been on the booze for about a month, solid. He's been holed up in his house, relying on friends to bring him carry-outs when its been too much for him to leave the house himself. That's all changing.

A couple of days have passed since Martin has been able to get a hold of someone, and he's beginning to feel like shit. No one will answer their phone. He can't get a hold of anyone to bring him drink. He's not thinking clearly and feeling a bit confused.

Here's what a normal alcohol withdrawal time frame looks like:

First 12 hours: During this stage, an alcoholic will feel strong cravings and may experience headaches.

Depending on the severity of their habit, they may also vomit or feel painful stomach cramps.

'Fuck this shit,' thinks Martin, 'I'm gonnae have to drag my carcass to the fuckin shop and get some booze. I canny handle this.'

Martin hasn't eaten properly in weeks. He can't remember the last thing he ate. This has been a bad one. The boozing has gotten way out of control.

'Fuck knows how long I've been on it this time,' thinks Martin.

12-48 hours: Heading into the first day, the alcoholic will start to feel feverish. Their body temperature will increase, their heart will pump faster, and they will feel increasingly anxious. It is common when withdrawing from alcohol to experience confusion during this time.

Through his hazy thoughts, Martin manages to dress and clean himself up a bit. This has taken tremendous effort, and he's not feeling good. He knows the score though, and if he doesn't get some booze into himself soon, things are gonnae get pretty nasty. It's not Martin's first time in this predicament. In the back of his mind, hiding away behind all the confusion and mist, he knows of the horrors that may come to visit. Withdrawal from the amount of booze hess been consuming is a serious matter.

Martin gently closes the door behind him as he attempts to make it to the 'carry-out' shop. The street looks quiet enough, 'so far so good,' he thinks. 'I'll head round by the golf course, cut through the wood and keep a low profile.' Martin makes his way through the woods toward the golf course shortcut.

48-72 hours: By this point, withdrawal delirium will set in. If the alcoholic is at risk for delirium tremens, the symptoms will begin to appear. They

may experience seizures, hallucinations, or strong shakes. This is considered to be the withdrawal "peak" and, if the addict is not treated properly, they may die during this phase.

Walking through the woods, Martin has almost made it to the golf course.

Martin   going going

Martin   going going

Martin has gone to the land of the DTs.

'Who the fuck is that shouting on me,' he thinks. 'Can't see any fucker. The sky looks a funny colour.'

'Martin, we're up here.'

'What?' 'What the fuck are you's doing up the fuckin trees?' He sees (in the hallucinogenic world that he has now entered) six of his friends perched on the highest branches of a group of trees.

'We've just climbed up for a bit of fun; C'mon up ya madman.'

This sounds like a great idea to Martin. He shouts up to his friend John,

'You seem awfully high up there, John. Is it an easy climb?'

'It' a piece of piss,' replies John, 'C'mon up.'

Martin starts his attempt to climb the tree only to hear Dunc and Linda shout from the other trees.

'Before you climb up, Martin, gonnae go get a ladder from somewhere, Linda's stuck up here and wanting down.'

'Nae bother Dunc, I'll nip along to they hooses and see whit I can dae.'

At this point on the golf course, four local guys are playing the hole next to the trees that Martin is shouting at. They, of course, can only see Martin because, in the real world, Martin is the only one there.

'What the fuck is this lunatic up to? Should we go over an check what's happening with him?

'Nah, leave the fuckin nutter alone.'

Martin heads over to the nearby houses, searching for a ladder to help one of his imaginary friends get down from the treetops, all logical in Martin's mind. He's moving from the hallucinogenic to functioning human and back to the hallucinogenic stage very quickly. He really does think that he's helping someone out by fetching a ladder. After chapping some doors and having no success, he approaches the next house, which has a large driveway.

Martin

going going

         Martin   going   going

Martin enters DT world again.

Two men are standing in the driveway, watching

Martin as he approaches.

'Alrighty,' says Martin. 'Could you help me out here by lending me a ladder? One of my friends over there, up the trees, is stuck?'

The nastier looking of the two turns to Martin and says,

'You' better fuck off right now, pal.'

Martin is feeling very uncomfortable with the man's attitude. The sweat is lashing from him, and he has noticed that the sky has gone a strange colour again.

'No need tae be like that pal, I'm only tryin tae help someone oot.'

As Martin turns and walks away, he senses danger. He thinks he hears one of the men whisper,

'Let's do him.'

Martin feels panic wash over him. He turns to see one of the men pull an enormous shiny meat cleaver from inside his jacket. Martin takes off, fuckin terrified.

'What the fuck, I was only askin for a ladder an this cunts wantin tae chop me up, run for fucks sake.'

Like Usain Bolt, Martin runs like fuck. He doesn't dare look back for fear of tripping over and being caught and chopped. The trees are whizzing past him. He doesn't remember ever being able to run this fast. He can hear the fuckers behind him shouting,

'Catch that bastard, chop his head off.'

Martin ain't stopping for nobody. He has his house in sight, and he's gonnae make it home and get the door locked behind him.

He bursts through the front door in blind panic, forgets to shut it, and bolts up the stairs. Nothing is gonnae stop his quest for safety. He opens the top hall cupboard, and like a gymnast, he's up the door and in through the attic hatch. He puts the hatch back in place and stands on it with all his weight; he's made it. He breathes a sigh of relief.

Just at that, he hears the two guys enter the house. 'What the fuck?' 'Shhhhuuuu,' Martin tries to quietly catch his breath as he listens for the would-be assailants' next move.

'The bastards up in the attic,' he hears them say, followed by the sound of footsteps coming up the stairs.

Martin's heartbeat is pulsating through his body and beating in his ears; his chest is banging like a drum. The sweat trickles down his face. He feels it running down his legs, running down his arms, his back. 'Don't faint now, for fuck's sake; these bastards will chop me up.' He feels the attic hatch moving; they're tryin tae force their way up into the attic. Martin pushes on the beams above his head and puts all his weight on the hatch. 'Don't let them get up here; whatever happens, don't let them get up here with that cleaver.'

Time passes. How much? Martin has no idea. There's been no attempt on the hatch for a while. 'Have they gone?' Martin listens for any kind of noise; his senses are on alert; he feels wired to the moon. Not a sound, no movement. He decides enough time has passed and opens the hatch. He knows that he must proceed with caution. Martin dreepies down from the attic. Coast seems to be clear.

He stealthily descends the stairs and enters the living room where his Da is sitting watching tv.

'Da, where the fuck did those two guys go?'

His Da can see that Martin is not in good shape.

'What two guys would that be, Martin?'

'Two guys Da, one wi a fuckin meat cleaver, they wanna chop me up because I wanted tae borrow a ladder tae help get Linda doon fae the trees. John an Dunc an awe them are up the top of the trees at the golfy.'

Martin's Da knows the time has come to call for the doctor. Martin's friend John died long ago, Dunc an Linda moved away about three years back. The hallucinations are mighty strong this time.

His Da calls the doctor.

Martin goes back up to his bedroom. He's feeling confused about what's been going on, and he knows that he's feeling very ill. Martin has a seat and tries to work out what's happening.

'Vee vish ya a merry Christmas.'

Martin hears a distant German-sounding voice.

'Vee vish ya a merry Christmas.'

'Where the fuck is that coming from,' thinks Martin?

'Vee vish ya a merry Christmas.' Martin looks around his room, no tv on, no radio on. The voice becomes louder now, more Demonic sounding, still with a German accent.

'VEE VISH YA A MERRY CHRISTMAS, VEE VISH YA A MERRY CHRISTMAS. VEE VISH YA A MERRY CHRISTMAS. VEE VISH YA A MERRY CHRISTMAS. VEE VISH YA A MERRY CHRISTMAS, VEE VISH YA A MERRY CHRISTMAS, VEE VISH YA A MERRY CHRISTMAS, VEE VISH YA A MERRY CHRIST-MAS...
....
....
....
....VEE VISH YA A MERRY CHRIST-MAS...
....
.... VEE VISH YA A MERRY CHRISTMAS.'

On and on, the voices in Martin's head go.

'VEE VISH YA A MERRY CHRISTMAS, VEE VISH YA A MERRY CHRISTMAS.'

Martin presses his hands against his head, pleading with the voices to stop.

'VEE VISH YA A MERRY CHRISTMAS.'

'What the fuck is happening to me? It's the middle of summer; what the fuck is going on?'

'VEE VISH YA A MERRY CHRISTMAS.'

On and on, it goes. Martin starts to bang his head off the table, pleading for the voice to stop. On it goes,

'VEE VISH YA A MERRY CHRISTMAS.'

Martin knows now that this is part of the horrors associated with severe alcohol withdrawal. During this little moment of clarity, Martin remembers being advised to focus on something, a distraction of sorts.

'VEE VISH YA A MERRY CHRISTMAS.'

He moves to the bathroom, where running a bath seems like the perfect distraction.

'VEE VISH YA A MERRY CHRISTMAS.'

Martin turns on the bath taps hoping to drown out the Demonic German voice playing on a loop in his head.

'VEE VISH YA A MERRY CHRISTMAS.'

The water starts to flow from both taps. He sticks the plug in, allowing the bath to fill.

'He thinks a fuckin baths gonnae help him, he thinks a fuckin baths gonnae help him, he thinks a fuckin baths gonnae help him.'

Martin now realises the bath taps are talking to him.

'He thinks a fuckin baths gonnae help him, he thinks a fuckin baths gonnae help him, he thinks a fuckin baths gonnae help him.'

'Fuck this'! He turns the taps off and runs from the house.

'VEE VISH YA A MERRY CHRISTMAS,' leaves with him.

Martin heads to the local reservoir, an area he knows well, hoping to find some peace. He's lost all track of time, and darkness has arrived.

'VEE VISH YA A MERRY CHRISTMAS, VEE VISH YA A MERRY CHRISTMAS.'

He walks around the reservoir through the night, resting here an there on the randomly placed wooden benches.

'VEE VISH YA A MERRY CHRISTMAS' plays on loop in Martin's head throughout the night.

The plan is to wait for Bob's shop to open at six, plead with Bob for a bottle of whisky, get a good drink inside himself and restore some balance to this fuckin nuttiness.

Six o'clock arrives, and Bob opens the shop to find Martin at the door. Bob knows Martin and has seen him in many bad conditions, but Bob is startled by how terrible Martin is looking. Martin pleads for the whisky; Bob knows the score and helps Martin out by giving it to him.

Within the hour, they find Martin laying on the pavement, unconscious, the empty bottle by his side. It's the police who have found him; they've been looking for him since late last night after Martin's Da had phoned them.

An ambulance is called.

Martin regains consciousness in the hospital. Looking around, confused, trying to work out where he is, and why? He notes all the tubes entering his arms, a few wires connected here and there. Monitors are beeping away at the side of his bed. There is also a nurse; 'a guard' thinks Martin. 'What the fuck is all this about.'

going going

Martin   **going going**

Martin's DTs return.

He sees the hospital wall open to reveal a Rastafarian disco.

'Martin wat u wan ting, wat u drink?'

The place is full of the most beautiful Jamaican women that Martin has ever cast eyes on. They are all dressed in magnificent colours, long swaying robes all shining in the disco lights. Each woman is prettier than the last. The one behind the bar that has poured Martin a drink and is shouting over to him is the personification of beauty. A goddess in the flesh.

Martin cannot believe his luck. 'I'm having some of this,' he thinks as he starts to pull at the tubes and wires attached to him. John, the nurse, is up like a shot.

'Martin, Martin, what's happening, my friend? Talk to me.'

'It's all good,' says Martin, 'I'm having some of this.'

He has a serious attempt to free himself as John tries his best to calm him.

'Get the fuck away from me. I'm going over to join that disco, an your no gonnae fuckin stop me.'

John, the nurse, walks to the wall and starts to bang his palms off the wall. 'This is just a wall, Martin; you're hallucinating.'

'It's no a fuckin wall. It's a disco full of beautiful women. Listen, mate, I know you's need tae make some money oan the side. This is as good a side-line as ave ever seen. I'm having some of it.'

Martin's last words, as the emergency doctor arrives to sedate him,

'What time's this nightclub open til?'

Delirium Tremens: A dangerous (but preventable) condition.

Unfortunately, the DTs are a potential reality for some drinkers. After all, alcohol is a powerful drug. No one plans to become addicted to alcohol, but many of us find ourselves slowly slipping into a

battle with addiction. Before you know it, you're unable to withdraw from alcohol without experiencing these life-threatening symptoms.

Luckily, however, Delirium Tremens is both curable and preventable. All you need is the right type of support. https://www.evergreendrugrehab.com

SERIOUSLY ILL

Invasive Endocarditis-infection of the inner lining of your heart chambers and valves. Left lung collapsed. Low blood pressure. Kidneys are failing, and sepsis. Martin has indeed not been looking after himself. His family are told that it's unlikely he will survive through the night. If he makes it through, the doctors will decide if he is saveable.

Martin somehow fights through the night with no idea what is going on with his life. He opens his eyes to see about ten people with white coats on, doctors, consultants, experts of all kinds deciding if it's possible to save his life. Martin can hear the proceedings; he can't speak, he's not sure why? He hears the prognosis, and it's not good. For the first time, Martin is hit by the seriousness of the situation. This is life or death.

Mr. Pathe seems to be the leader; Martin can see and hear him speak to each doctor in turn. Martin is terrified.

Mr. Pathe turns and looks directly at him. Martin

knows this is it. The next decision that Mr. Pathe makes will decide his fate. Martin tries to plead for his life. He doesn't want to die. He wants another chance at life. He wants to clean up, sober up. At that moment, Martin wants life, not death. He can't speak, can't move, 'Must have me drugged up,' he thinks to himself. He tries to plead for his life with his eyes. Martin looks directly back at Mr. Pathe, begging for his life. Everything stops, time stops, there is nothingness. Mr. Pathe says,

'Let's get Mr. Bisley to the Jubilee hospital, now, save this man before it's too late.'

Martin starts to cry.

His family are informed and advised to get to the hospital. It's all go. Martin will be taken to the Jubilee, and everything possible will be done to save his life. He is getting his chance. Can he take it?

Martin is aware now of what's happening. He's been given a chance. His family are all around him, wishing him well as he is wheeled from the ward to the awaiting ambulance. It's happening fast, into the lift, out through the hospital, up into the ambulance, transferred onto the ambulance bed. This is it, heading to the I.C.U.

'God help me. Please.' Martin prays for the first time in his life.

The flashing blue lights are on. The siren is on. The ambulance pulls away at speed. This is indeed life or death.

Martin is thrown violently against the rear doors of the ambulance. They haven't strapped him in! The nurse is banging through to the driver.

'Stop the fuckin ambulance. He's been thrown against the doors.'

Martin's nightmare continues.

The driver pulls over and comes back to help strap Martin in.

Theatre lights, shiny things, chest getting shaved. The attempt to save his life begins.

He goes through two 8-hour operations, receives a new aortic valve, gets a couple of stents put in, and some other minor stuff is taken care of.

Martin survives.

He spends 17 days in hospital recovering his strength. During this time, he is sectioned under the mental health act and kept under supervision.

What a journey it's been for Martin. As he sits across from me, sipping his coffee, telling this story of mayhem. He reminds me that all this took place a few years back and clean living is now where it's at.

PROCEED WITH CAUTION

6. DON'T JUDGE MY SCAR

I open my eyes; here we go again, another day. I say, 'Thank you.' To whom or what? I don't know; I just say it as I appreciate the fragility of life. With that in mind, I go to the kitchen and put the kettle on, stare at it while it heats up, and try to untangle myself from the remnants of the strange dreams from the night before, wondering what today will bring. I don't give this as much thought as I used to; it is more out of habit that it still comes into my consciousness as I have concluded that it's pointless trying to predict anything. Life has a mind of her own. She will direct an episode of Quantum Leap with me as the leading actor if she sees fit. I call it 'The Absurdity of Life.'

It takes about four coffees to psyche myself up for what may unfold, it started with one cup, but that was a while back. I carefully make the coffee, trying not to spill anything, and head back to my bed. I turn my phone on and thus begin the daily ritual I have been practicing; it consists of texting 'Good Morning' to my group on WhatsApp, which includes family members and friends.

Three coffees down, and I start to feel a bit fresher. With the caffeine kicking in nicely, I take advantage and head to the bathroom, where I turn on the tap at the sink. As I lift my head, I see my reflection in the mirror, and sometimes I don't recognise the person looking back at me. He looks much older than I am, greyer than me, and has a few more wrinkles than I do. It is a weird feeling. However, one thing that I always see which never changes is the scar on my face. I can't remember how long it has been there; it's been there for years, well, a good few anyway.

That's all it takes for my brain to go off on a tangent.

'What do you expect each morning? Do you think one day your gonnae wake-up and the scar will have miraculously disappeared? What did you use to think when you saw scarred people?'

I can't remember what I used to think. I don't like to think that I was judging people that I knew nothing about, attaching stories to them that were made up in my head.

Was I quite judgmental about people's appearances before I got my scar?

Aren't we all a bit judgemental?

Is that an innate human trait to judge? Are we pre-programmed with prejudices, or do we learn them along the way?

I wonder if people make judgments about me when they see my scarred face? Do I even care anymore about that kind of shite, other people's opinions? What kinda fuckin world do we live in now anyway?'

And on it goes…

I can tell it's gonnae be one of those days where my mind wants to take me back and replay over and over that stupid day.

Here we go…

Back in the days of heavy drinking and drug-taking, it always created an environment where mayhem was possible, especially the way we would go at it. If you've been out bingeing with some hardcore friends on day two or three, things can get a bit fuckin confusing.

My brain's off on another tangent,

'What starts these fuck ups? What does it take for things to spiral out of control when you're fucked out of your barnets? I think about this for a while and conclude that it doesn't take much.

It all seems so stupid now looking back. One of the boys had been slowly but steadily getting louder and louder, becoming more boisterous. I think he had been snortin a bit more coke than he usually did, maybe drinking more spirits too. I wasn't doing too well either, downing the spirits and whatever else was going around.

Everyone's head must have been fried at this stage in the game. That's probably why we started shouting at each other. That's what I remember, raised voices, nasty things being said. All completely out of character due to the situation, too much drinking, and drugs. The tension building, the shouts getting louder, then that's it. The first punch was thrown, and the mayhem began. I remember rolling around on the floor, fighting for what felt like my life. This was a serious fuckin opponent, fucked out our heads or not. This was a dangerous situation. I remember feeling scared; holy fuck, this guy is as strong as anyone I've ever encountered. We're punching and kicking, head butting and biting. It's out of control. No one tries to pull us apart. It turns out they were scared too, said it was like two wild animals in the jungle.

We break apart.

I stagger to the kitchen. I know we're not done yet, not by a long shot. Round two will be beginning real soon. I throw some water on my face, catch a glimpse of myself in the mirror. That bastard has stabbed me in the face, cut me open across my chin. I'm enraged. I rush back to the other room to have my revenge. I'm on him again, punching, biting, whatever it takes. It makes me feel sad and dejected when I think of this, how out of control things got. Very sad, very sad indeed. There was blood every-where. It was horrible. I hate that day.

That's as much as I'm gonnae think about it today. I don't think about it much; on occasion, though, it appears like it has a force of its own. When I say that I don't think about it much, I don't think about that actual day. I don't want to think about it; it creeps into my thoughts when I'm least expecting it, like today, horrible.

The actual scar, though, that's become a thing of its own. Every day I catch a glimpse of my scar. Every day I catch a glimpse; it brings on mixed feelings. Feelings of bewilderment, what the fuck's this world all about? Feelings of sadness mixed with feelings of happiness and confusion. Most days, I feel like there is a hole in my soul.

What makes one person judge another just by a glance at them out in the street? I've learned to truly never judge a book by its cover, as they say. Always treat people with kindness as you have no idea of the journey they are on.

Mayhem is a possibility for all. If your life path leads you to occasional darkness, hopefully, you will find your way through. Some are luckier than others. We're all 'Jock Tamson's bairns,' they say.

Don't judge my scar, don't judge anyone. Take people as they are. I read somewhere something like; some of the most judgemental people attend church, whereas some of the kindest are covered in tattoos. It's along they lines; you know what I mean?

Life is too short for sure. One of my younger brothers passed away a few years back. I don't have the vocabulary to put into words how painful that is. To say that it's a life-changing event would be an understatement. On a good day, he was the kindest, most caring person you could ever meet. On a bad day, we all get them; he could be a bit boisterous.

I look at my scar again. That boisterous boy I fought with that day was my brother. I miss him every day. Don't judge my scar, don't judge anyone!

7. IRVINE WELSH, YOU'RE A BASTARD!

I bumped into 'Tam One Eye' the other day, and this is his story.

I close the book. *Dead Men's Trousers*, Irvine's latest offering. What a read; that was fuckin incredible.

'How dare you end it like that, you bastard Irvine Welsh!'

I'm sitting on a plane coming home from my summer holiday, and he ends the story in a way that crushes me with disappointment. No spoilers here. If you want to know what happens, you can buy a copy. More to the point, something in that story has got me thinking about the death of my friend. The drug they smoke, DMT, aka the spirit molecule, took Begbie to a place where he encountered the dead. This fascinates me, and I begin to wonder if there's a possibility that I can get some of this drug and meet my friend in the spirit world? I need to know what the fuck this all is about.

My brain is in overdrive, contemplating how to get my hands on this stuff. I wonder if I would be strong enough mentally to take it. What if I travelled to the spirit world and met him...? What would I say? That would be some wild shit indeed.

The plane lands, off we get, and I still can't stop thinking about this DMT, 'The most potent hallucinogenic known to humankind, I repeat myself, 'THE most potent hallucinogenic known to humankind. I need to get my hands on it.'

The first thing for me is to start with some research about this wonder drug and who has taken it? Find out everything I can about it. It turns out there's a documentary been around for years detailing the whole DMT experience. It goes into some detail about the entire procedure. I watch this a few times and decide I need to try this shit out, although more research is required.

'Who else is into this kinda stuff, and how do I get in touch with them?'

Joe Rogan's podcast turns out to be a wealth of information. He can't say enough about the drug, and almost every guest gets quizzed.

'Have YOU tried DMT?'

Joe shares some of his experiences, and it sounds incredible, as well as terrifying. A notable guest who had tried it on many occasions is the one and only Mike Tyson. Joe and Mike share stories about some of the entities in the spirit world and how they have encountered dancing jesters and mechanical elves. Crazy-sounding things like 'The Lego People' give

Mike Tyson advice and allow him to return with life-changing messages. Mike claims that the DMT experience has saved his life, mental stuff.

I was hooked. I knew it was now just a matter of time til I experienced the wild side involved with this drug.

I send a message to Irvine Welsh on Twitter. He thinks I'm asking about his recent book tour. I soon corrected that and let him know that I was interested in taking the drug DMT. All because of reading *Dead Men's Trousers*. In fairness to him, he puts a shout-out for me into Twitter world, asking If anyone can help this brother out with DMT? I get some responses, but nothing of any substance, no one offering me access to the drug.

What the fuck is my next move?

How am I gonnae get my hands on this? Since my friend's death, I had developed an interest in the afterlife, time travel, ghosts, anything really that could give me a chance of seeing him again; it was all fuckin mental. I wanted to see him again, and maybe this DMT drug was the answer.

A few weeks pass by, and I'm having no success with tracking down DMT. I'm carrying out plenty of research about the drug but can't get a hold of any. The more research I do, the more bizarre it all becomes.

There are indeed some crazy stories out there about how powerful this drug is and the places it can take you. I'm finding out that there is a debate in the land of hallucinogenic users. The big debate is whether, when you take DMT, do you travel to another dimension and visit another realm that exits out with, or does it all take place within your mind?

Hopefully, I'll be finding out soon enough.

What to do?

Fuck it. I've done enough research, and I can't get my hands on it. I'm not up to date with all the Snapchat and Instagram world, which I hear is the modern way to obtain drugs now.

I decide to make my own!

I begin to get as much information as possible regarding the procedure involved. Luckily I find a couple of well-made tutorials on YouTube, marvellous; we're on our way. Christ knows how many times I watch these tutorials; YouTube is brilliant for that kind of stuff. I mean, where else are you gonnae find a tutorial to make Dimethyltryptamine?

I make my list of ingredients and what type of cooking gadgets I need. I don't use the kitchen that often, so it's all from scratch. Mixing bowl, slow cooker, glass pie dishes, and on it goes. When it comes to the ingredients, most are pretty easy to source. A couple of chemicals here and there leave me needing to find the main ingredient, Mimosa Hostilis, the bark from the Jurema tree. I don't recall climbing any Jurema trees when I was little. It must be some sort of exotic tree from far away? It turns out to be fuckin miles away in... South America. Luckily the power of the internet wins again—Mimosa Hostilis, no problem, eBay, Amazon, whatever, just like that. Order sent, and now it's just a waiting game til my main ingredient arrives. It's starting to feel like this is becoming a reality, and it's now only a matter of time til I find out how mental this stuff is. Am I getting a little worried? Oh yeh, indeed, I'm worried, alright.

Postman's been, here we go!

I've watched the tutorials enough now that I know them off by heart; still, I'm gonnae set the laptop up in the kitchen and start-stop the instructions. Just to make sure I'm following everything correctly.

There's a wee dangerous part near the end when you're messing with fluid that's highly flammable, and there's a fair bit of heat coming off the rice pot, gotta be careful to keep the window open and get a good bit of ventilation on the go.

We're off and running.

I put the Mimosa Hostilis into the coffee grinder to get it all powdery, then it's into the mixing bowl, throw in some powdered chemicals, and away we go. I carefully put in the correct ingredients, and slowly my DMT cake begins to take shape. It's looking good. Right, next move, let's get this cake into the pie dish and follow the procedure. All the time that this is happening, I'm start-stopping the tutorial, making sure I'm following the instructions exactly. I want to get this right the first time.

Now my DMT cake is in the pie dish; I move on to the part with the rice cooker. I won't reveal all the cooking details here as I don't want anyone trying this at home, not unless you've done a lot of research. I do my first 'pull' on the cake using the highly flammable fluid which draws the DMT crystals out. At this point, I can only hope that I'm doing it right because we are gonnae have to wait til morning to find out. I put my result into the freezer compartment of my little fridge. I seriously doubt if there will ever be anything quite like this in my fridge again. I cover the pie. According to instructions, I will be back to complete more 'pulls'.

'Okay, okay.' I steady myself.

I get the place tidied up and head to bed. We're almost there; it's nearly DMT time.

I sleep well, although it does take me some time to nod off as I'm starting to realise that this DMT (the most potent hallucinogenic known to humankind) may just be waiting in my fridge. Well, it will be by morning.

THE DAY OF RECKONING

As soon as I'm awake, there's no hesitation about where my mind wants to go. Instantly my thoughts are on the DMT trail. I leap out of bed and rush through to the kitchen. The first signs are good; everything is still here; nothing has exploded during the night. I open the fridge, then the little freezer part, and gently lift out my prize. I tip the fluid to one side (this type of fluid doesn't freeze in domestic freezers), and there it is, I've done it. I have made the spirit molecule. Well, I hope that's what it is because I will be trying it out later when it dries properly. I put the fluid into a wee jar as I'm not done with that yet; I will use it again in cake 'pull' number two. I then set the pie dish out to dry near the window as it still requires good ventilation at this stage in the game. That should be ready to try later.

Now, who can I get as a wingman to aid me in this interesting adventure?

I give Brian a call, aka 'the Juke,' or 'Juka'. We sometimes call him Russell because he's always telling folk that Russell Crowe will play him when the time comes to make a movie of his life story. He's damaged a few brain cells over the years, just like the rest of us, I suppose.

'Alright, Juke, what's happening?'

He's had a few cans of beer at this point, nothing too much; he is still communicating reasonably well.

I explain to him that I've been experimenting with making a drug that I have been researching.

I then tell him that I have successfully made it in my kitchen and want to try it out, but I need his help.

'I need a wingman, someone to back me up with this experiment. Are you up for it?'

'C'mon roon,' he says.

I head roon.'

I sit down on his couch and unpack the accessories required for this possible trip to the twilight zone. I don't tell him too much about it, just that it's a hallucinogenic type thing. I don't want to frighten him by revealing it's one of the most powerful drugs known to humankind (I'll tell him that later).

'Ok, my man, this is what I want you to do. When I set this up...

I point to a container thing I made (courtesy of You-Tube tutorials again) and then continue my spiel.

'Ah'm gonnae heat this bottom bit. The container is gonnae fill with smoke, and you're gonnae take the lighter out of my hand. Then I'm gonnae take the wee earplug out the hole in the jar, put my mouth to the hole and suck the smoke into my lungs.'

'Then what?' he asks.

'Well, I'm no that sure what happens next. I'm assuming you may have to take the jar out of my hand or something. I dunno. Maybe I'll drop the jar. I've no idea. That's when I leave the situation in your capable hands.'

'Okay,' he says, 'as long as my hoose doesny get wrecked, I'll go along with this fuckin nuttiness.'

I prepare the jar.

We are ready to go. I'm a bit nervous, more than a bit. I'm fuckin terrified, but that's ok; I'd be more surprised if I wasn't as we're moving into unchartered waters here, way into unchartered waters. I run through all the possibilities with the Juke of what could go wrong. If I drop the lighter, do this. If I drop the jar, do that. If it turns out that I haven't made it correctly and things don't look too good, get me an ambulance. I ask him if he can do CPR, he laughs as he thinks I'm joking.

HERE WE GO...

I hold the lighter under the jar and start to heat the powder. The smoke begins to fill the void, and I know it's time to pass the lighter to the Juke. I slowly remove the earplug I've used as a stopper, put my mouth to the hole and draw the acrid smoke into my lungs. I vaguely remember knowing to take my face away from the jar. I think I may have indicated somehow to the Juke to take it, or he just sensed that I was on my way and knew to lift the jar from my hand. As I went to sit back, reality as I had known it, just disappeared.

(Now, obviously, I'm writing this with hindsight and having had some time to reflect. I don't have the vocabulary that I would like to have. I also don't have the writing skills that I would like to

have. However, I'm gonnae have a bash at trying to give some kind of description about what happened)

In the blink of an eye, I had left this world. I mean instantaneous, like someone or something had touched a button on my shoulder. I don't know how to describe the way sound had altered, but it had changed. A sound I'd never heard before began to reverberate around my head. As I looked up, the room had liquified. Were we suddenly underwater? This was not the room I had been sitting in with the Juke. I had entered a white chamber that felt like some kind of waiting room.

I remember feeling scared by the power of what was happening. Strange writings and pictures with weird types of hieroglyphics start to appear all around me in 3D. I hear a voice telling me to close my eyes and sit back. I've no idea where the voice had come from. I follow the instructions and close my eyes.

Then...

Boom!

I've entered a cosmic wormhole; that's the only way I can describe it. On each side of me is a dancing jester, yip, a dancing fuckin jester! I don't know how I know, but I know that they are my escorts to see me through this wormhole.. We start to travel through it at speeds unimaginable in earthly terms. The wormhole wall is covered in art, languages, ancient tribal designs, architecture, and everything is on overload. There's way too much to try and take in; it's overwhelming. The colours are breath-taking, the designs are exquisite. As I travel further along with my jester escorts I get scared again and stupidly open my eyes. I wouldn't recommend this as that was even more frightening. Eyes closed again, and we're back hurtling through this wormhole. I kinda remember at one point having thought along the lines of, 'Ah, so that's why they built those things.' It was just mesmerising what was on display.

The direction I'm travelling tries to change a little. We seem to be heading slightly downwards into a deep red section. I don't like the feeling that this is bringing and somehow manage to steer back into the main thoroughfare of the wormhole. The walls of the wormhole start to show some change. In between all the incredible sights on display, sets of eyes begin to appear. I see some of the eyes appearing more than once; it's as if they are following me down the wormhole, viewing me from the other side. It's fuckin crazy stuff. I start to hear some weird sounds then voices saying,

'Here he comes, yes it's him, he's coming.'

It feels like THEY have been expecting me.

Who the fuck are THEY?

Then whoosh! I've catapulted out the wormhole, the dancing jesters have gone, everything has gone dark, and it feels like I'm looking upwards into a dark void. How long have I been traveling? Where the fuck am I? Then a voice.

'Welcome.' That's what I hear next.

'Welcome.'

I look up in this dark void to see the appearance of what I can only describe as the personification of female beauty. A face of indescribable feminine perfection looks down at me. It feels like an all-encompassing power like I'm in the presence of mother nature or something, Mother Enya? I don't even know what Mother Enya means? She then says,

'Welcome back; we've been awaiting your return.'

'What? Welcome fuckin back! Have I been here before?'

I thought I might have remembered if I'd been to somewhere as exotic as this. When I say that she says welcome, I don't mean as we would understand it. It's all some sort of thought exchange, telepathic type stuff for want of a better description.

I'm wondering where the fuck we are going next as my body, or whatever form I'm in, begins to rise upwards like something out of the old Highlander movie. This Mother Nature or Enya uses a force of sorts to ascend me to what feels will be another level where untold revelations await about the origins of time, space, and life itself.

I'm looking up at this Mother Enya? Only her face is

visible and is surrounded by a whooshing, whirling, wispy forcefield of immense power.

She is the boss around here.

I'm rising toward this incredible scene when suddenly I start to kinda shudder. I'm thinking, 'What the fuck is that shuddering? ' I know that sounds a bit odd after travelling down a cosmic wormhole with dancing jesters and whatnot, to be concerned about a shuddering. But that's how it was, I thought to myself, or not to myself as the case was in this insanity, '

'What the fuck is shuddering?'

Mother Enya proceeds to let me know that I've not to worry, I've just not taken enough DMT to proceed any further at this point, and she looks forward to when I return. I'm fuckin shittin you not, that was the message. I slowly descend into the dark void, gently lowered until I touch what feels like something solid, and everything changes again. I'm able to open my eyes, and I have returned to planet earth. I'm back on the Juke's couch.

'What the fuck just happened to me?'

(I could have stretched that story out considerably, but I'm just tryin to give you a flavour of what happened).

Juka sees my eyes open and instantly asks how it went.

'How was it?' 'Did you see any colours?'

Did I see any fuckin colours? I'm thinking to myself, 'How the fuck am I gonnae try to explain this?' I jump up from the couch and stand in the middle of the room with my hands over my face. I'm in shock. I can't believe what's just happened. Everything I've read about the DMT is true. I've just travelled to another fuckin dimension or something. I don't know where I've just been. WTF happened there? 'Holy fuck, man.' I don't know what to think or say.'

'Juke man, that was some trippy shit man, really fuckin far out man.'

That's all I can say at that moment. I'm bewildered or something. I don't know. There was too much happening during the experience to even begin to comprehend what the fuck just went on there? There's an exhilaration attached to the bewilderment. I have just been somewhere, but where, 'What the fuck?' I'm freaked out a bit. I had read it was strong stuff, but I hadn't expected to travel down a cosmic wormhole. What had I expected? Fuck knows?

'Did I see any colours?'

'Juke, my man, I don't know how to explain what just happened. I feel as if I've been allowed to glimpse the unknown. I know that sounds fuckin mental, but what happened to me there was deep. 'There's something out there, my man, really fuckin far out. A spirit world or some other dimension exists beyond the veil of reality as we know it. What the fuck does that sound like? Fuckin nuts, that's what it sounds like, but it is what it is.'

Awwwwww, Juka is looking at me like my time has finally come, and it's maybe his cue to make the phone call and get me signed in to Gartnavel Hospital.

'Listen, Juka, I wouldn't know how to explain properly about what just happened, but I've got an idea... there's enough of that DMT left for you to have a blast.'

Juka thinks about it for a few seconds...

'Fuck it, set it up. I'm going in.'

'Ok, Juka, all I'm gonnae say is, don't keep your eyes open at the beginning because it's fuckin frightening.'

That's all I say. There's not much point saying anything else as he's gonnae find out real soon for himself.

We get it set up.

'Are you all ready to go, Juka?'

Thumbs up, we are ready for blast off...

He draws in the smoke, closes his eyes, and gently lays back on the couch. I watch him as his head starts to move about, jerking from side to side erratically. He looks like he's trying to talk to someone. He's mouthing words; I can't hear what he's trying to say. I shudder to think what he may be encountering. His arms are up in front of him as if he's trying to fend something off. I hope he's alright, wherever he's gone. I see him smiling, and he seems to be ok. I wonder if he might actually be enjoying himself.

(Before I go further with the story, I just want to add that Juka has never heard of this drug before. He has no idea what others have experienced when under its influence. He has never seen any documentaries about South American retreats or watched any Joe Rogan podcasts, and we haven't had any previous discussions about what may happen when you take this drug. I want to clarify this because I don't want anyone to think that some of these hallucinations can be pre-programmed. What I'm trying to say is, I have no influence on what Juka may encounter as you're about to find out.)

Ten minutes pass as Juka squirms about his couch and then just suddenly stops. There's no movement for about a minute, and then his eyes open. He sits up, looks right at me, and says,

'What the fuck is that I have just taken? What the fuck have I just experienced?'

I ask him if he's alright and tell him he was away for about ten minutes or so.

'What happened, Juka? Did you see any colours?'

He starts to laugh,

'Did I see any colours, no wonder you didn't answer me when I asked you that? I was away for ten minutes. How is that even possible when I was travelling through a timeless universe? I closed my eyes right away as you had told me, then suddenly, I'm hurtling through the universe in a fuckin spaceship of sorts. At first, I thought I was in a spaceship, and then I realised I was the spaceship. I was travelling through the universe at speed I couldn't begin to explain. There was no ship! I was hurtling through a timeless universe like some time traveller. Shapes, dimensions, holographic faces, art. WHAT THE FUCK?'

He starts to get a wee bit panicked and begins shaking a little. I calm him down.

'Juka man, breath man, you just had a deeply spiritual experience, of course, you're gonnae feel a bit weird.'

The cans of beer he had earlier seem to have worn off rapidly.

'What else did you see?'

He says, 'This next bit is gonnae sound a bit strange.'

'How's it gonnae sound a bit strange after talking about travelling through the universe at supersonic speeds?'

'Well, I'm travelling as fast as fuck, and suddenly, over on my left appear all these little like, Lego people, wee mechanical elves or something. How fucked up does that sound?'

'It sounds alright to me, you bastard. I can't believe

you got to see the mechanical elves! I wanted to see them as I've been reading about them.'

'What the fuck are you talking about,' he asks. 'You've been reading about them? Do you mean that other people have seen these fuckin same things?'

'Yip, I've read that the mechanical elves are popular in the DMT realm. What were they doing?'

His reply will stay with me forever. He says,

'Remember, I was travelling too fast through the universe to engage, but I saw hundreds of them as I flew past, and they were all laughing at me and giving me the middle finger.'

I ask him to repeat that, then say,

'I bet you didn't think you were gonnae make a statement like that when you woke up today?'

But you're a lucky bastard that you got to see them.'

'Seriously though.' he says, 'What the fuck is that I took? I've taken some mad stuff in my time, but nothing like that, man. That's some powerful fuckin shit, and you're telling me that...

You made this in your fuckin KITCHEN!!!'

'I certainly did Juka. Thank you for being my wingman today. Til next time my friend?'

There's no doubt about the power of this DMT. It's pretty frightening. The possibilities of where one

may travel to and what one may see are endless.

Are the hallucinations generated from within one's psyche? Are the hallucinations a journey to another realm that exists beyond our earthly dimension? Is the spirit world a destination, and DMT opens a portal? These are questions. Who has the answers?

DMT

In ancient times, The Creator wanted to hide something from humans until they were ready to see. The Creator gathered all the animals and sought their advice. "I want to hide something special from the humans until they are really ready for it; it is the realization that they create their own reality." The Eagle said: "Give it to me. I will take it to the highest mountain and keep it there." The Creator replied: "One day, the humans will conquer the highest mountain and find it." The Salmon said: "Give it to me. I will take it to the deepest ocean and keep it there." The Creator replied: "One day, the humans will explore the deepest depths of the ocean and find it." The Buffalo said: "Give it to me. I will bury it in the heart of the great plains and keep it there. The Creator replied: "One day, humans will rip open the earth and find it there." All were stumped until Little Grandmother Mole, who lives within the heart of Mother Earth and sees with her spiritual eyes (not her physical eyes), spoke up: "Why don't we hide it inside them? That is the last place they will look." The Creator smiled knowingly and said: "It is done."

~ Sicangu Lakota Oyate ~ (An Old Sioux Legend)

'Sometimes you eat the bear, and sometimes the bear eats you. It is all the soul experiencing life.'

8. TO INSANITY AND BEYOND.

(PART 1 OF THE 'YOUNG RAB' SERIES)

In this story, we are going to spend some time with young Rab. Young Rab's in trouble and finds himself in the trenches fighting the ravages of addiction. His drugs of choice are alcohol and cocaine, a formidable combination in the slow descent into darkness and down the slippery slope.

We catch up with Rab as he is enjoying some kind of cosmic dream.

In Rab's dream world...

The battle was raging in the cosmic wormhole. This was the battle of all battles. I had slain Thoth in one-to-one combat. The challenge that he had put out had been accepted, and he had lost. The Goddess Bastet had fled after that; she had changed dimensions. I had tracked her, though, kept tabs on her. That problem would be dealt with in due course. In the meantime, this battle had to end. At this stage, I was untouchable; the energy I had received from the decapitation of Thoth had been immense; any window of opportunity the demonic forces from this realm had of defeating me had long gone. Word had spread amongst the soldiers that I had slain Thoth; his army was at the point of surrender. I saw no reason for any more unnecessary deaths. I would accept the surrender and allow his troops to join with me; it would be fine, it always was.

Paul's armies were fighting in the fourth dimension; it wasn't too much of a problem; all was well under control. I could call upon him any time during these demonic battles, as he could me.

The days when the Gatekeeper had kept the peace had long since gone. His army of jesters (strangely named as these were fierce characters) had gone into hiding with the mechanical elves. The mechanical elves, builders of the human race, had fled as Thoth and his armies had come through the wormhole. (There they are again, those jesters and elves, maybe Rab has puffed the DMT?)

I would restore order in this realm, back to the times of peace and harmony; there had been too much darkness in recent times. Firstly, I must find this Goddess Bastet; she slipped through the wormhole and broke the guidelines. Yip, there were guidelines and honourable ways even for demons to conduct themselves; but this fucker was off and running, trying to somehow save herself from what was coming.

Me, I was coming to finish this fucker, one way or another. She would still have some choices, as is the nature of these realms. She could join me, forever in my debt, my demonic slave; perpetual silence would be her forfeit. Or she could take the honourable way out for defeated demons and consume herself; this would at least allow her soldiers to move on with honour. Bastet must destroy herself and her host. She had taken a human host; we knew where, though. She had shown herself once, by mistake, a few years back, in earthly terms. In wormhole dimension time, she had only just vanished.

As word travelled throughout the realm of perpetual darkness that Thoth was dead and the Goddess Bastet had fled, the dark forces were falling into line. They would be reprogrammed and brought to the cause of life.

I must deal with Goddess Bastet in earth time. I will travel through the wormhole to establish how far she has gone to ground and work out what fate awaits her...

Young Rab slowly awakens...

'What the fuck was I dreaming about? Thoth, wormholes, fourth dimension? Whoa, my head hurts. Oh no, don't tell me I've done it again. Where the fuck am I? Whose fuckin clothes are these I've got on? No, no, no,

'I'm in a caravan?'

'Fuck's sake, what have I done this time?'

Rab surveys his sleeping quarters. Yip, he is definitely in a caravan and has clothes on that he does not recognise. He also realises that he has some aches and pains, which make him think he has most likely been in some kind of fight. He looks at the scratches and cuts on his arms. This is not good. He feels the lumps on his head and discovers one of his eyes is almost swollen shut.

'Fuckety fuck fuck. What can I remember?'

I went up to see Stuart and was gonnae help him with some work. That bit's crystal. Ok, we started with a bottle of Desperado each. A wee quick beer that turned into four or five, then I started talkin my usual shite. Clear so far.

'Oh no, there's the moment!'

I see Stuart's whisky collection staring out at me from his cabinet.

"Stuart, do you fancy pouring some whisky from that beautiful collection you have?" Stuart, being the lovely guy he is, obliges me, and we get into whisky. No work would be getting done, that's for sure.

I can remember up til that bit, and then it starts to get a bit hazy...

I've got a vague recollection of being in a car with Stuart's wife; where was she taking me? Something in the distance is ringing a bell in my head. Ian, I've headed to Ian's house. Then there's nothing coming back to me; I'm drawing a complete blank, total blackout, then I've woke up here.

'What the fuck was that dream I was having?'

Fuck it. There are more pressing matters to be dealt with rather than wondering about some daft nutty dream. What carnage have I been involved in again? I'm fuckin sick to death of these blackouts and this binge drinkin. How much debt have I gotten myself into with the coke this time?'

'AAAAAAAAAAAAAAAAAAAARGH!!

'HERE WE GO AGAIN!'

Time to take a couple of deep breaths and begin the process of trying to piece this nonsense together.

I brace myself and leave the caravan. I head over to Stuart's house to no doubt begin my apologising routine and find out if anyone's talking to me. Also, try n find out what's happened.

A couple of chaps to the door, and Stuart appears.

'Jesus Rab, how you feeling, my friend? I hope you don't feel as bad as you look. For Fucks Sake. What the fuck happened to you last night after my wife dropped you off at Ian's? You were right out your dial.'

'Stuart, I'm fuckin sorry mate, if I've caused any bother. I've got a complete blackout after leaving here. I vaguely remember being in the car with your wife, and then I woke up in your caravan with these clothes on?'

Stuart brings Rab into the house and makes some coffee.

'Listen, Rab. I'm not giving it to you tight; I like you, we're good friends, but for fucks sake maman. After you were dropped off, we thought no more about it. You'd obviously had a few. You were guzzling the whisky like water. I did think to myself at the time that's gonnae catch up wi him. Anyway, I'm in bed sleeping, and I get wakened up by the sound of someone, well, no someone, turns out it was you shouting like a fuckin madman. Then it just stopped. By this time, I'm laying fully awake, wondering if I'd really heard anything. Susan turns to me and says, "That sounded like Rab shouting".'

I thought fuck it and pulled some clothes on and went outside to see what the disturbance was and found you laying on the middle of the road with just a pair of trousers on, fuck all else. You were bleeding and mumbling something about wanting to kill people. I couldn't get any sense out of you, so I brought you inside, and we cleaned you up as best we could. You didn't want to be taken to the hospital for a check-up. We didn't know what to do with you, so we put some fresh clothes on you and stuck you in the caravan out the way to let you sleep it off. I would have put you on the couch, but we were up sharpish to put the kids out to school.

'Christ Stuart, I feel fuckin ashamed,' says Rab. 'I'm so grateful for your help, and I canny thank you enough. I know I've got some problems, and I'm trying to deal wi them. Without much fuckin success, it seems. Saying that, I'm no takin a kicking off anyone, though, that's for sure. I wanna find out what the fucks went on. Who the fucks gave me this sore face? I'm gonnae give Ian a phone and see if he can shed some light on this mess.'

'I'm with you on that Rab; if someone's taken a liberty with you in that condition, let's get it sorted.'

Rab phones Ian and tries to find out what's gone on during his drunken rampage. Ian is a little bit annoyed with Rab and tells him that he was out of order, and says he's never seen him like that before.

'You turned up at the house like a savage, right out your fuckin mind, demanding that I let you in, and we get some booze and coke sorted. I had to tell you that it wasn't happening as I had some people round for dinner, and you weren't getting in because you were just too far gone and tryin to cause problems.' Rab asks about how he is all bruised and battered.

'You best come see me, Rab, and I'll tell you what happened.'

Stuart grabs his car keys, and they head down to Ian's to find out the finer details of this latest catastrophe.

They arrive to find Ian waiting at the front door.

'Here's what happened, Rab. You arrived at the hoose smashed, and I've telt ye ye canny come in. I've got my brother and his partner o'er for dinner. You're out your fuckin mind. You seem to take that on board and stagger away. I shout after you to be careful and go straight home. Then I'm sitting at the dinner table: me, my wife, the two kids, and my brother Scott with his partner. The patio door curtains are open; we're sitting at the table enjoying our dinner with a bit of chat on the go; next thing you know, you come charging up the back garden; you've got no top on and run face-first into the patio doors. Like a madman, I mean face-first right off the glass!

'I've never seen anyone act like that. You were screaming like a man possessed and just bounced off the glass. We were sitting there like, did that just happen? Then you gets back up, staggers back down the garden, and charge the doors again. Face first, right off the fuckin glass again and bounced back into a heap. We thought you'd knocked yourself out. Fuck knows how the glass didn't smash. No wonder you're all cuts and bruises, man. Look at you – one of your eyes is almost swollen shut. You must feel like shit!'

Ian was looking at him, shaking his head.

He continued, 'At that point, my brother Scott went out to see what the fuck was going on with you while I tried to calm everyone down in here. It was fuckin bedlam man. Scott gets you off the ground trying to see how badly you've hurt yourself, and the next thing you know, you're fighting him, throwing punches, and tryin tae bite him. What the fuck had you been taking? Scott had to punch you a couple to get you to back away, and then you just took off. You ran back down the garden, fell over the back fence, and disappeared into the night. All the time this was happening, you shouted all kinds of threats about everyone getting murdered. Jesus Christ Rab, what's happening to you?'

Rab is fuckin mortified.

'Ian, I can't apologise enough, mate. I'm so ashamed of my behaviour to the point that I can't handle what's happening here. I canny handle what I'm hearing, and I am ready tae burst oot greeting. I don't know whit tae dae here, man.' He looks around at Stuart, who can't believe what he's hearing either, and says:

'Stuart, please just gonnae take me hame til I rest up and try tae get maself sorted. I'll be back, Ian, to make things right with everyone who was seated at that table.'

Stuart drops Rab at his flat after they had picked up some provisions to see him through the next couple of days as he tries to get himself together. Rab locks the door behind him, lays down on the couch, and starts to sob uncontrollably.

Rab's head is fried. He knows that this shit can't continue. These blackouts and fuck ups are happening way too regular now. Laying here just sobbing his heart out ain't gonnae solve a thing. He hears his phone ringing. It's Ian on the other end.

'Listen, Rab; it's just to let you know that it turns out one of the kids filmed what happened on their phone. You know what kids are like these days, Rab. Well, I'm giving you the heads up because word is that it's getting shared on social media. They filmed you running at the doors, topless, smashing your face off the glass. From what I've just been told, they've slowed down the second time you ran at the doors and added music in the background, *Chariots of Fire*. I'm sorry, Rab, obviously I'll have a word wi them about it, but it's out there, mate.'

Rab disconnects the phone and sinks further into the darkness of depression. All he can think of is this video reaching a million views on YouTube...

Rab spends the next two days and nights sweating it out on the couch. He goes back and forth, in and out of sleep. There are times when he's not sure what is awake time and what is dream time? His what is now becoming a recurring dream about Thoth and other dimensions is also frying his mind. He tries not to think about his most recent adventure with the patio doors. He begins to wonder if it really happened or is it just shit he's making up in his now very fragile mind. He's confused and not that in touch with reality as all the booze and coke slowly drips out his system.

In moments of clarity, he becomes overwhelmed with waves of depression. His life is in freefall, and he feels lost and doesn't know which way to turn. His cold-turkey-style withdrawal exacerbates all this.

As he moves past day two of his so-called sorting himself out, he decides that he can't handle any more of this. Laying here with the sweat lashing out him, and fuck knows what going through his head, he decides the journey to healthiness will have to wait.

'Fuck this; I need to get back on it,'

His decision is made. He convinces himself he needs something to take the edge off of this fuckin craziness. He washes, gets ready, and heads out to a local house where he's always welcome. I guess you could call it a kind of sanctuary for people who are in that lifestyle. This house is always open, and there's never any judgement here – as long as you're buying. There's always coke for sale, and booze too!

For once, he feels that the gods are on his side because it's dark, close to about ten o'clock. This suits Rab just fine and dandy as he is less likely to bump into anyone who may know him. Less chance of anyone seeing his sore face, less chance of anyone seeing the state he is in withdrawing cold turkey from the booze and coke for the last couple of days. A thought flashes through his mind of the possibilities surrounding the video of him running at patio doors face-first actually being a real thing. He's not sure what's real anymore. He pushes this thought away.

Almost at the house now, sanctuary.

'Ah, welcome Rab, come in, come in. you're not looking too well, big fella. Here's a beer, get that down ye an you'll be fine. I take it you'll be wantin to purchase some coke to gie yersel a wee lift?'

There are a few bodies scattered throughout the house. Rab knows everyone who frequents this place. Are they friends? Well, that's anybody's guess. Some may be friends, but one would never know as all connection is through a haze of drink and drugs. Rab pays for a bag of coke and a bottle of Jack Daniels, then settles down at the table where three of his associates are seated and well on their way to being smashed out their tiny minds. After a couple of meaty lines of coke and a large Jack Daniels threw back in a oney, Rab starts to feel human?

It's party time again.

The booze and cocaine are doing their thing, and the place is livening up. There's music on in the background. A couple are having a wee slow dance in the middle of the living room. A lot of loud chat is coming from the kitchen. Rab and his associates are at the table, all trying to talk over each other, thinking that their patter is worth hearing far more than the shite everyone else is talking.

Rab's in full flow, regaling everyone with tales of deed and daring, most of it being absolute shite magnified tenfold by the effects of booze and drugs, of which by now, he has consumed plenty of. Rab feels fuckin marvellous; he's finished the first bag of coke, so he orders up another. As he's given the second bag, it's accompanied with a little whisper in his ear just where he's at with his tick bill, a wee reminder.

No fuckin problem to Rab. His bill sits at four hundred. Even by Rab standards, he knows the lines of coke that he's been sniffing have been large – really fuckin large! As Rab swigs another Jack Daniels, he feels bulletproof and has escaped all the bullshit that had been torturing him as he lay on his couch earlier. 'Fuckin bring it on,' he thinks; 'This is the way to go.'

'Right lads, geeza minute till I nip for a pish and I'll tell ye the end of this story, you need tae hear it, it's fuckin quality.' Rab goes to the toilet and locks the door behind him. He struggles to pee as the coke is pulsing through his body. After a few minutes of straining, Rab gives up with the idea as it's just no happening. He wants to get back in about it and finish telling his mates the incredible story he was halfway through. As he goes to leave the toilet, Rab suddenly doesn't feel too clever. The vision in his good eye, the unswollen one, feels a bit off.

He has a look at himself in the mirror. 'What the fuck?' He knows that his face is bruised and battered from the patio doors a couple of days earlier (he's now accepted that this happened and not something he's dreamed up). What's going on here with his good eye, though? The pupil in his one remaining usable eye has decided to jam inwards. It's peering tightly at his nose. He can't see right, and it won't straighten out no matter what he tries. He starts to panic a little.

He manages to unlock the toilet door and make his way back into the living room.

'Hey lads, what the fuck's happening wi my eye here; can yous see it's jammed inward?'

Well, that's all they need to hear and see. Laughter erupts from everyone. Uncontrollable laughter as they are all out of their minds, and this just happens to be the funniest thing ever.

Rab stands there his face all battered and bruised with his one good eye deciding that it wasn't playing anymore and was taking the rest of the night off. He can't see clearly, but he knows they're all rolling around the floor in fits of laughter at his predicament.

'Fuck you all, he shouts, I'm havin a situation here an a don't need all you cunts laughin at me, it's no fuckin helpin the situ.'

From amongst the laughter, someone shouts out,

'That's what I hear happens when you've got a brain tumour.'

Now the laughter is louder than ever, the loudest laughter that Rab has ever heard.

'A fuckin brain tumour.'

His mind, or what's left of his mind, latches onto this thought and won't let go.

'A fuckin brain tumour. A fuckin brain tumour! Huv a got a fuckin brain tumour?'

He hears another shout,

'Take a line of coke, an you'll be brand new bigchap.'

'Brand fuckin new,' thinks Rab; 'huv I got a brain tumour?'

Panic sets in Rab's head as he makes for the door to get away from this mess. It's three in the morning as he runs along the street, wondering how far it is to the local hospital.

Rab arrives at the hospital as his mind slowly starts to dissolve into insanity and beyond.

To be continued...

You, yes you. You feel a bit confused? How do you think Rab feels?

What happens to Young Rab in the hospital?

Does he continue sliding down the slippery slope into the darkness?

What will the next fuck up be like?

Will he decide enough is enough and seek help?

We will catch up with him again, real soon.

If you know of anyone who may be struggling with addiction, addictive behaviours or mental health issues. Be supportive, be there for them. Be kind.

Thank you for taking the time to read this book

But before you go...

I want to share a piece of wisdom that has helped me many times in my journey of life...

Never, ever...

ever...

.

ever...

ever,ever,ever fry sausages in the nude.

'Always Love'

Don't Believe Everything You Read !

'Heroes take journeys,
confront dragons, and
discover the treasure
of their true selves'

-Carol Paterson

'The day I decided that my life was magical, there was suddenly magic all around me'

-Marbeth Quinn.

Proceed with Caution

This book contains stories of hallucinogenic happenings inter-twined with alcohol, and drug abuse. There is violence and darkness-all in with a sprinkling of Scottish humour.

I dare you...